Title: A Chainsaw Maintenance Pocket Guide!!!

Subtitle: Basic Care For Stihl & Husqvarna Chainsaw(s)!!!

Introduction:

In the vast expanse of the world of trimmer tools, where the steadfast hum of carbureted engines echoes through time, a delicate dance of maintenance and care unfolds. It is a realm where the art of preservation meets the science of operation, where seasoned hands know that the key to unlocking the full potential of these machines lies not only in their operation but in the meticulous upkeep they demand. While some may view these tools as relics of a bygone era, the truth remains that with proper maintenance, a trimmer can serve faithfully for years on end, a trusty companion in the ever-changing landscape of tasks and challenges.

Chapter 1: The Foundation of Care

In the first chapter, we lay the groundwork for a successful maintenance routine. We delve deep into the intricate anatomy of your trimmer, exploring each component's function and significance. From the engine to the cutting chain, understanding the inner workings of your tool is essential to nurturing a symbiotic relationship with it. Furthermore, we emphasize the importance of establishing a safe and organized workspace, ensuring that every maintenance task is executed with precision and care.

Chapter 2: The Dance of Prevention

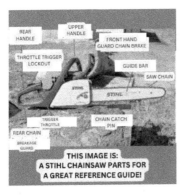

THIS IMAGE IS: A STIHL CHAINSAW PARTS FOR A GREAT REFERENCE GUIDE!

Preventive maintenance is the cornerstone of a healthy trimmer. In this chapter, we embark on a journey through the realm of proactive care, exploring the various measures you can take to keep your trimmer running smoothly and efficiently. From regular inspections to timely replacements of wear-prone components, we equip you with the knowledge and tools to preemptively tackle common issues before they escalate into costly repairs and unexpected downtime.

Chapter 3: The Symphony of Lubrication

Lubrication is the lifeblood of any mechanical system, and your trimmer is no exception.

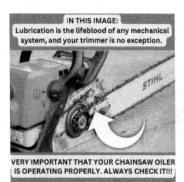

IN THIS IMAGE:
Lubrication is the lifeblood of any mechanical system, and your trimmer is no exception.

VERY IMPORTANT THAT YOUR CHAINSAW OILER IS OPERATING PROPERLY. ALWAYS CHECK IT!!!

In this chapter, we delve deep into the art of proper lubrication, guiding you through the process of selecting the right oils and ensuring that every moving part is adequately protected and nourished. From the engine bearings to the cutting chain, we unravel the intricacies of lubrication maintenance, empowering you to keep your trimmer in optimal working condition.

Chapter 4: The Ritual of Cleaning

A clean chainsaw is a happy trimmer, and in this chapter, we explore the transformative power of regular cleaning. We guide you through the best practices for removing debris, dirt, and grime that can compromise your tool's performance and longevity. From the air filter to the cooling fins, we shed light on the importance of meticulous cleaning and maintenance, ensuring that your chainsaw remains a beacon of efficiency and reliability in your arsenal of tools.

Chapter 5: The Song of Renewal

Even the most well-maintained chainsaw will eventually require parts replacement. In this chapter, we embark on a journey through the process of identifying worn-out components and replacing them with care and precision. From spark plugs to air filters, we guide you through the intricate art of part replacement, empowering you to breathe new life into your trimmer and sustain its peak performance for years to come.

Chapter 6: The Legacy of Safety

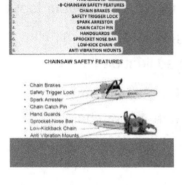

CHAINSAW SAFETY FEATURES

Safety is paramount in the world of trimmer maintenance, and throughout this book, we intersperse valuable safety tips to ensure that you and your tool emerge unscathed from every maintenance task. From proper protective gear to safe handling practices, we equip you with the knowledge and awareness to prioritize safety in every aspect of trimmer maintenance.

Chapter -7: Is your chainsaw having trouble staying running?

Refer to Our Guide to Pinpoint The Issue.

Encountering a situation where your chainsaw suddenly stops while you are in the middle of a task can be frustrating. To address this problem effectively, it is essential to understand the potential factors causing your chainsaw to malfunction. By referring to our guide, you can identify and troubleshoot the issues hindering your chainsaw from running smoothly.

Numerous issues can impede the operation of your chainsaw, ranging from a faulty spark plug to a dirty air filter. Common culprits include a damaged fuel line, poor-quality fuel, or incorrectly calibrated high-low adjustment screws. Additionally, more complex problems such as a malfunctioning carburetor or engine compression issues can also lead to your chainsaw failing to stay running.

Below, you will find a breakdown of the most prevalent problems that may be preventing your chainsaw from running continuously. The guide also offers suggestions on how to address these issues and when it might be necessary to seek professional assistance.

If your chainsaw won't remain running, consider the following simple explanations:

1. Old Gas / Bad Fuel: Gasoline can degrade over time, leading to inefficient combustion and potential engine stalling. Using fresh fuel with an octane rating of 89 or higher is recommended, especially if the chainsaw has been inactive for an extended period.

2. Fuel Delivery Problem: A clogged fuel filter or damaged fuel lines can disrupt fuel flow to the engine, causing performance issues. Regularly checking and replacing the fuel filter can help maintain proper fuel delivery.

3. Clogged Air Filter: A dirty or clogged air filter can restrict airflow to the engine, affecting its operation. Cleaning or replacing the air filter as needed can help restore proper functioning.

4. Clogged Exhaust: A blocked spark arrester can impede exhaust flow, leading to engine stalling. Regularly inspecting and cleaning the spark arrester can prevent this issue.

5. Clogged Fuel Tank Vent or Fuel Cap: Blocked vents can disrupt fuel flow and cause engine problems. Ensuring proper ventilation within the fuel tank is essential for optimal engine performance.

6. Blocked or Damaged Idle Port: Debris or damage to the idle port can impact airflow, affecting engine operation. Cleaning or replacing the idle port as necessary can help resolve this issue.

7. Bad Spark Plug: A faulty spark plug can hinder engine starting and performance. Inspecting and replacing the spark plug if necessary can improve engine operation.

8. Clogged or Broken Primer Bulb: Issues with the primer bulb can affect fuel delivery and engine performance. Replacing a damaged primer bulb can help maintain proper engine function.

Additional Causes of Chainsaw Stalling Issues

In addition to the previously mentioned issues that can typically be resolved without professional assistance, there are more intricate problems that necessitate specialized knowledge and skills.

Carburetor Adjustment - Fine-tuning the Idle, High, and Low Screws

As your chainsaw's engine and components wear down, the carburetor may require adjustment. This adjustment involves utilizing three screws on the chainsaw to regulate the engine's airflow properly. However, adjusting the carburetor is a challenging task. Each chainsaw model has specific settings, and tuning the engine by ear can be quite difficult for an untrained individual.

When the engine receives either too little or too much fuel from the carburetor, it can result in stalling. Chainsaws are equipped with screws for adjusting airflow during idle, low-speed operation, and high-speed operation.

If your chainsaw stalls when revving up or fails to reach its maximum power, you should adjust the high-speed screw. For stalling issues during idle, the idle screw needs adjustment. And if the problem occurs at low speeds, the low-speed screw requires adjustment.

It is essential to bear in mind that adjusting these screws alters the air-fuel ratio of the engine. If the fuel mixture is left too lean or too rich, it can significantly damage the engine. For this reason, it is advisable to seek professional assistance from a service shop for carburetor adjustment issues.

Compression Troubles

If your chainsaw is old, experienced lubrication problems, is challenging to start, or has exhibited decreased power, it may be beneficial to conduct a compression test.

Ideally, a healthy engine should display a compression level of over **70 PSI** for a small saw, while larger engine saws should have at least 100 PSI. Compression tester gauges are readily available in the market for conducting this test. You can perform the test yourself or opt to have it done at a specialized shop. Low compression levels in your chainsaw's engine can indicate internal damage, such as faulty piston rings, crankshaft seals, or a cracked piston. Repairing such damages can be costly and may signal that it is time to consider purchasing a new chainsaw. Therefore, conducting a compression test before investing in expensive parts like a new carburetor is advisable.

Dirty, Blocked, or Faulty Carburetor

After confirming that all other components are functioning correctly, it is essential to inspect the chainsaw's carburetor. A clogged carburetor can lead to engine stalling or a failure to start. Attempt to clean the carburetor using a carburetor cleaner. If this does not resolve the issue, consider removing the carburetor for a more thorough cleaning using an automotive carburetor cleaner.

For individuals with the time and patience, purchasing a carburetor rebuilding kit is an option. This kit includes worn-out or damaged components, along with fresh gaskets and O-rings. After cleaning and rebuilding the carburetor, reassemble it and test the chainsaw's functionality. If the chainsaw operates correctly, then your efforts have paid off.

If the chainsaw still does not function properly, it may be necessary to replace the carburetor if it is irreparably damaged. In such cases, opting for a new carburetor may be a quicker and easier solution, albeit at a higher cost. When replacing the carburetor, remember to acquire new gaskets for sealing between the carburetor and the manifold. Additionally, replace the fuel filter and add fresh gasoline to ensure a clean and efficient start.

Always refer to your chainsaw's user manual for essential information regarding regular maintenance requirements, as well as other crucial instructions for the machine's upkeep and your safety.

For more complex issues that require specialized knowledge, such as carburetor calibration or engine compression problems, seeking professional assistance may be necessary. Proper maintenance and timely troubleshooting can help keep your chainsaw running smoothly and efficiently.

The Art of Troubleshooting

No maintenance journey is without its challenges, and in this chapter, we delve into the art of troubleshooting common issues that may arise during the care of your trimmer. From starting problems to chain tension issues, we guide you through the process of identifying and resolving issues efficiently, empowering you to overcome obstacles with confidence and skill.

As we reach the culmination of this odyssey through the art of trimmer maintenance, remember that the care you invest in your tool today will pave the way for a future of reliable performance and longevity. By following the practices outlined in this comprehensive guide with diligence and care, you will unlock the full potential of your trimmer and ensure that it serves as a steadfast companion in your endeavors for many seasons to come. So, dear reader, let us embark on this journey of maintenance together, as we unveil the secrets behind efficient chainsaw care and embrace the art of nurturing and preserving your trimmer tool with passion and dedication.

Taking care of your chainsaw isn't always easy. In this part, we'll talk about how to fix common problems you might have with your trimmer. Whether it won't start or the chain is too loose, we'll show you how to figure out what's wrong and fix it. This will help you solve problems on your own with confidence.

As we finish this guide on taking care of your trimmer, remember that the time you spend on maintenance now will help your tool work better and last longer. If you follow the advice in this guide carefully, your chainsaw will work great for a long time. So let's learn how to take care of your trimmer together. We'll show you how to keep your tool in good shape and make it last for years to come.

Under The Engine Cover

In the rugged world of chainsaw maintenance, precision is key. As the dawn breaks, and the forest stirs with life, a seasoned lumberjack knows that every component of their trusty chainsaw must be finely tuned for the day's challenges ahead.

1. The Ritual of Preparation: Adjusting the Mixture Control Lever
As the sun peeks over the horizon, the first step is crucial. Adjust the mixture control lever to full choke, a ritualistic gesture that shields the combustion chamber from the invading dust and debris of the forest floor.
2. The Dance of Cleansing: Tapping and Blowing Life into the Air Filter

With a steady hand and a focused mind, tap the air filter on a solid surface, coaxing out the dust and woody debris that cling to its fibers. A gentle blow, like a whisper on the wind, frees the filter from its burdens without causing harm.

3. The Art of Preservation: Protecting the Micro Pores

Beware the temptation of tools that scrape and scratch, for they threaten the sanctity of the micro pores within the filter. Let nature's breath flow freely, unobstructed by the scars of impatience.

4. The Elixir of Longevity: Applying Air Filter Oil

For the chainsaw that yearns for longevity, a dose of air filter oil prescribed by the manufacturer is a balm of protection. Let it seep into the fibers, a shield against the elements that seek to corrupt.

5. The Symphony of Reassembly: Securing the Air Filter

As the cover plate beckons, ensure the air filter is embraced in its rightful place with a tactile click that resonates through your fingers. Only then may the cover plate be fastened, completing the symphony of reassembly.

6. The Vigil of Protection: Adjusting the Mixture Control Lever Once More

Before the chainsaw roars to life, the mixture control lever must again be set to full choke, a guardian against the unseen foes that lurk within the combustion chamber.

7. The Caress of Caution: Handling the Spark Plug

With gloved hands, approach the spark plug with reverence, for it bears the heat of the chainsaw's heart. Only the brave dare touch its fiery core.

8. The Language of Color: Interpreting the Spark Plug's Hue

In the flickering light of the forest clearing, behold the spark plug's hue. "Cardboard brown" speaks of balance and harmony in the dance of fuel and air.

9. The Clues of the Spark Plug: Decoding the Signs

A spark plug veiled in black soot whispers tales of richness, of fuel in abundance. A white spark plug cries out for more, for the hunger of fuel unmet.

10. The Ritual of Renewal: Polishing the Electrodes

With grit and determination, polish the electrodes with fine sandpaper, cleansing them of the burdens of combustion. A toothbrush and a touch of fuel breathe life back into the spark plug's essence.

11. The Touch of Restraint: Threading the Spark Plug. As the spark plug finds its home within the engine, remember the touch of restraint. Fingertight is all it needs, a gentle embrace that wards off the specter of overtightening.

12. The Final Embrace: Reuniting Spark Plug and Boot. With a click that resonates through the forest, reunite the spark plug boot with its mate. Only then may the chainsaw awaken, ready to face the trials of the day.

In the heart of the forest, where the trees whisper ancient secrets and the chainsaw's song echoes through the canopy, mastery awaits those who heed the call of maintenance. Unveil the secrets, embrace the rituals, and let your chainsaw sing with the power of a thousand forests.

Under The Cover Plate

Beneath the Cover Plate: Clear away any debris that has built up inside the cover plate of your chainsaw. It's not crucial to be extremely thorough unless you're planning to store the chainsaw for a long time without use. Check the chip deflector to ensure it's in good shape and properly attached to the cover plate. Inspect the bar nuts on the cover plate to make sure they are securely fastened and not at risk of coming loose.

The chain catcher plays a vital role in safety by preventing the chain from hitting your right hand and arm if it comes off the bar unexpectedly. Make sure the chain catcher is present, securely attached, and in good condition. Replace it with a new one if needed. The tiny e-clip may seem insignificant, but it is crucial for holding all the components beneath the cover plate in place. When reinstalling the e-clip, determine which side has rounded edges and which side has sharper edges. Position the e-clip so that the sharper edge faces outward towards the cover plate for a secure fit in the axle groove. To ease reinsertion, use the open end of your scrench to guide the e-clip into place, preventing it from getting lost. Once in position, rotate the e-clip gently to ensure it is correctly seated and secure on all contact points.

Reassembling Under the Cover Plate

- When putting the parts back together under the cover plate, ensure that the washer is reinserted with the inner recessed portion facing outward towards the cover plate to provide extra security for the e-clip.

- Check and replace the sprocket if the drive link grooves show excessive wear, and ensure the replacement sprocket matches the correct number of drive link grooves for your chain and bar setup.

- Insert the sprocket correctly with the branding facing outward towards the cover plate, and verify the chain brake's functionality by engaging and disengaging it to ensure proper contact with the clutch drum.

- Clean any debris between the chain brake and drum to allow for full engagement, and remove any grease that may have accumulated inside the drum.

- When reseating the drum, ensure that the notch on the bottom edge fits around the oiler worm to enable proper oiling of the chain and bar.

- Listen and feel for a light metallic "click" to confirm that the drum is seated correctly around the oiler worm, and check by twisting the drum to ensure it is engaging the oiler worm.

- Be aware that over time, the drum may wear down the oiler worm due to the necessary slight movement when seating the drum, causing eventual shearing of the oiler worm. If you notice that the oiler worm is not engaging properly even when the drum is correctly positioned, it is important not to operate the saw until a professional can replace it. Operating the saw without the oiler worm engaged will cause the oil pump to function unreliably, resulting in inadequate lubrication for the chain and bar. This can lead to excessive heat, potentially causing the chain to seize and the bar to warp.

Next, inspect the needle bearing by spinning it around to check for any micro cracks. If you discover any signs of cracking, it is crucial to replace the needle bearing immediately. Prior to reinstalling the needle bearing onto the axle, it should be degreased with a manufacturer-recommended bearing grease. While there is some debate regarding the amount of grease to use, it is generally safe to apply a slightly larger amount.

One method to ensure sufficient grease is to cover one end of the bearing with a finger and then fill the bearing completely with grease until the "needles" are pushed outward. Slide the bearing back onto the axle, allowing any excess grease to be pushed out. You can use your finger to spread this excess grease around the outer part of the bearing once it is fully in place on the axle.

To clean the guide bar of your chainsaw, start by clearing out the grooves using a tool like a raker guide. Remove any oily or woody debris by sliding the tool from the sprocket towards the oil ports. This method helps prevent debris from clogging the nose sprocket. Use the tool to also clear any debris from the oil ports located on each side of the bar. Check the straightness of the bar by looking down its length with one eye, inspecting from different angles to ensure accurate assessment without being influenced by light.

If you notice any burrs or curled edges, use a flat or bastard file, or a dedicated bar file, to smooth them out. Pay close attention to the area around the nose and sprocket, where curled edges commonly occur due to chain slap. It is normal for wear to appear around the edges of the bar, eventually causing the paint to wear away. However, be on the lookout for any discoloration, particularly a bluish tint. A bluish hue indicates that the steel's tempering has been compromised, necessitating the replacement of the bar with a new one.

Don't forget to flip the bar each time you maintain your saw to ensure even wear on both sides and prolong its life. Grease the nose sprocket if you have a grease injector, but it's not necessary every time you service the chainsaw. Using compressed air lightly at the end of the day should keep it spinning freely. When tensioning the chain, aim to point the bar's nose upward as much as possible to cut with the bottom of the bar. Tighten both bar nuts alternately, ensuring the one closest to the throttle is fully tightened first to secure the bar in place. Avoid over tightening the nuts; they should be secure but still easily loosened if needed.

Chainsaw Maintenance Guide

Regular maintenance is essential to keep your chainsaw running smoothly and efficiently. By following a comprehensive maintenance checklist, you can ensure that your chainsaw remains in good working condition, performs optimally, and has an extended service life.

This guide provides detailed steps for maintaining your chainsaw, covering daily, weekly, and monthly maintenance tasks to keep your machine in top shape.

Daily Maintenance:

By following this comprehensive maintenance guide and performing regular checks and tasks, you can ensure that your chainsaw remains in excellent condition, operates safely, and serves you well for years to come.

What do you need to do to keep your chainsaw running smoothly? How do you maintain your chainsaw? What do you do if the chain won't stop? If you are grappling with these questions, this is the perfect generalized guide for you. It is not brand specific, although we based the content on maintenance guides and schedules suggested by manufacturers.

The maintenance procedures we recommend here will keep your machine in good running order and extend its serviceable life. Because not all machines are equal, our guidelines may not match your machine. Therefore, we urge you to compare it to the maintenance procedures recommended by the manufacturer. An authorized service workshop should carry out the more extensive work not covered in this book.

You'll have to regularly check to ensure your chainsaw is safe and in good running order; and that your chain is sharp. It is my experience that using a checklist is best to ensure I don't forget or neglect something. I always tend to "forget" things I should have done, it's if my mind just focuses on the job, ignoring the maintenance tasks. Therefore, I share this list with you.I tailored the maintenance checklist to someone who uses the chainsaw daily. If you use your chainsaw less often, you may adjust the weekly and monthly schedules to suit you.

Daily Maintenance

- Clean the outside of the machine. Remove the covers and clean them, then set them aside.

- Operate the choke lever to close the choke butterfly valve, it will keep the dirt out of the carburetor when you clean the filter. Use a shop blower to clean the machine.

- Clean the chain brake band and ensure it operates safely. You will test it again before you use the machine.

- Remove the chain, bar and clutch cover

- Make sure the lubrication hole in the bar is clean and open. Clean the lubricant feeder hole that delivers the oil to the bar, make sure it is open.

- Clean the bar groove and inspect it for wear. If the bar has a sprocket tip, lubricate it with the correct bar grease. The tip grease holes are on both sides of the bar. Grease both.

- Every time you sharpen the chain, flip the bar over. It helps them wear evenly.

- Check the saw chain regarding visible cracks in the rivets and links. Make sure the saw chain is not stiff, and check the rivets and links for abnormal wear, replace a worn, stiff chain.

- If you notice that the chain is not sharp, sharpen it and check its tension and condition. If you feel unsure, follow our section "How to sharpen the chain".

- Check the chain drive sprocket for excessive wear and replace when necessary.
- Make sure that the chain catcher is undamaged and securely in place and replace it when required.
- Remove the air filter and clean it as recommended in your manual, use a clean rag to clean the carburetor air intake port.
- Assemble everything.
- Check the engine, tank and fuel lines for fuel leaks.
- Check that the throttle control and lockout work safely. The throttle lockout must prevent the throttle from working if you do not depress the lockout. When using the throttle control, make sure its action is

smooth, and it always returns to the idle position immediately when released.

- Assemble the machine and adjust the chain. You correctly adjusted the chain if you can lift it about 3/8 inch at the top center of the bar. The chain must move freely by hand with no binding.
- Make sure you lock the bar tightly and ensure that all nuts and screws are tight.
- Inspect the underside of the bar to make sure it's getting sufficient oil and correct any errors.
- If you find that the stop switch sometimes fails you, it's time to check it. It may need cleaning out.

Weekly Maintenance

- Check the starter for wear and clean it, oil the center bearing.

- Check the starter cord for frayed edges. Remove the assembly and check the return spring.
- Check that there is no damage to the vibration damping springs or rubbers and replace if needed.
- Lubricate the clutch drum bearing.
- Clean out the cooling fins on the engine and the impeller, and the cooling slots in the cover, etc.
- Use a piece of wood and clean out the bar grooves and file away burrs from the edges of the bar.
- Clean or replace the muffler spark arrestor screen.
- Clean the carburetor compartment and the air filter. Replace if required.

Monthly Maintenance

- Check the chain brake band for wear and replace it when worn down to less than 0.024 inch at the most worn point.

- Check the clutch center, clutch drum and clutch spring for wear and clean all components. Oil the center bearing.

- If you use the chainsaw daily, clean the spark plug and check that the electrode gap is 0.020 inch.

- Clean the outside of the carburetor and check for fuel leaks.

- Check the fuel hose for cracks or other damage and replace a hardened or cracked hose.

- Empty the fuel tank and clean the inside if dust accumulated, especially around the filler area. Clean the filler filter.

- Empty the oil tank and if you feel dust or debris inside, clean the inside by flushing it with mineral spirits.

Chapter 8: How to Sharpen the Chain

 To keep the chain sharp, some companies recommend that you use a file to sharpen the cutting teeth frequently, even daily. Professional loggers say they wait till the chainsaw slows down somewhat. Filing the chainsaw blades often makes the job easier, but it seems like a waste of time to them. They often use more than one chainsaw and they buy chains in bulk and assemble them. It's not the same for homeowners that only need a chainsaw for yard maintenance and *cutting firewood*. The

reality is that a chainsaw chain needs sharpening on a consistent basis. Most users tend to sharpen their teeth when the chips become mixed with sawdust.

Put the chainsaw bar in a vise or secure it to prevent any movement while working. You will see YouTube movies of guys supporting the chainsaw on a log, but I consider that as roughing it. I recommend that you secure the chainsaw properly so you file safely and without rounding the cutting edge. To ensure that you sharpen every tooth at the correct angle and just enough to hone the edges, you must secure it.

- Engage the chain brake to keep the chain steady.
- Sharpen the cutting teeth first. Position the file depth gauge on the chain so that

the arrows on the gauge point towards the chainsaw bar nose.

- File at a right angle to the chainsaw rollers.
- File every other cutting tooth using a smooth and even pushing stroke with a slight upward pressure on the file.
- Turn the saw around to face the opposite direction.
- Finish filing the other cutting teeth using the same motion as before.

 **How to Sharpen Overview**

- Put the file gauge over the depth gauge but be sure to use the "hard" or "soft" side depending on the wood you normally saw.

- With the file tip feel for the depth gauge to get a feeling for how much you need to take off.
- Remove the file gauge and file the tip of the depth gauge using one or two strokes and measure again with the file gauge. Never take off more than necessary. Rather be safe than sorry, if you remove too much, the teeth bite deeper and the saw becomes dangerous.
- When you feel satisfied that it's good, you round the edge of the depth gauge slightly to ensure the chain cuts smoothly.
- Finish filing the other depth gauges using the same procedure.

Fuel Tank and Fuel Lines

Make sure the fuel of your chainsaw is clean and not contaminated with water, dust or debris. Refueling is a task we often neglect because we are in a hurry to get back to the cut. Keep the fuel and two stroke oil in separate sealed containers and only mix enough for the task at hand.

Clean the area around the fuel cap before you refuel and clean the mixing jugs before you use them. Dirt is the main enemy of any internal combustion engine–keep it out. Mixing the oil incorrectly will harm the engine, be careful. Do not store fuel-oil mixes as these mixes may degrade with time and become inefficient.

Inspect the fuel tank, cap, fuel lines and carburetor for fuel leaks and repair it immediately. Fuel leaks are wasteful and could cause a fire or at least contaminate the environment.

Ethanol burns hotter than gasoline. It can cause the engine to overheat, and you will see the effect as worn plug electrodes. Use the recommended octane gasoline without ethanol when possible. If you cannot get ethanol free gasoline, it must contain no more than 10 percent ethanol.

Cooling Air Intake and Cooling System, Air Filter and Carburetor.

- All modern chainsaws have forced air cooling to keep the working temperature as low as possible.
- The cooling configuration comprises air intake fins on the starter cover, an air guide plate, and fins on the flywheel. The assembly blows the cool air over

the cooling fins on the cylinder, guided by the cylinder cover.

- Clean the cooling fins on the cylinder and the flywheel fins with a brush once a week. You may find that you need to do it more often in demanding conditions. Dirty or blocked cooling fins will cause the engine to overheat; damaging the piston and cylinder.

Carburetor Adjustment Screws

Your carburetor will usually have at least two settings; the L-jet to set the idling with, and the H-jet that sets the mixture at working speed. You adjust the idle speed with the supplied T-screw or a screwdriver that fits. With the carburetor adjusted correctly, the engine runs smoothly in every position and picks up speed without hesitating. The engine may four-cycle a little at its maximum speed.

It is important that the chain must not move when the engine is idling. If it creeps at idle, you reduce the idle speed a little till it stops. If you cannot set the carburetor correctly without letting the chain move, it is possible that the clutch needs a service. There must be a safe margin between idling speed and when the chain rotates.

If you set the L-jet too lean, it may cause starting difficulties and poor acceleration. At the other end of the range, if you set the H-jet too lean, the engine will have less power, poor acceleration and could suffer damage to the engine.

Properly adjusting the carburetor on your chainsaw is essential for maintaining peak performance, durability, and safety. While it may seem intimidating initially, understanding the process and following the steps carefully can make this task manageable, even for those with less experience. Here is a detailed guide on how to correctly tune a chainsaw's carburetor, incorporating expert advice and proven techniques.

Understanding the Fundamentals

Before fine-tuning your chainsaw's carburetor, it is crucial to grasp the basics. Most chainsaws come with three important adjustment screws - the low-speed, high-speed, and idle screws. Each of these screws plays a significant role in the performance of your chainsaw. To prepare for successful tuning, consider the following steps:

Ensure the bar and chain are properly attached and tensioned. Incorrectly fitted bar and chain can greatly affect carburetor adjustments.

The condition and correct placement of the air filter are critical as they directly impact the operation of the carburetor.

Before making any adjustments, run the chainsaw at idle and give it a few revs for approximately a minute to ensure it is at the correct temperature for tuning.

Prioritize safety when tuning your chainsaw's carburetor. Carry out the tuning process in a well-ventilated area to prevent the accumulation of harmful exhaust fumes, which

can pose health risks. Additionally,
acknowledge that chainsaws produce high
noise levels during operation, which can harm
your hearing over time. Wear appropriate
hearing protection to safeguard your ears while
being able to hear and respond to subtle
changes in the engine's sounds during
adjustments. This dual approach ensures you
protect your health while maintaining the
precision required for effective carburetor
tuning.

Adjusting the Screws

Understanding Limiter Caps

Many modern chainsaws have limiter caps on
adjustment screws to prevent users from
making extreme adjustments that could harm
the engine or make the chainsaw unsafe.
These caps allow minor adjustments, usually

about half a turn in either direction, providing room for fine-tuning while protecting the engine's integrity. If your model requires a special screwdriver, such as many Husqvarna models, you may need to visit a dealer.

Fine-Tuning the Low-Speed Screw

Mastering the adjustment of the low-speed screw is crucial for achieving an optimal fuel-air mix at idle, ensuring smooth operation and responsive throttle engagement.

The low-speed screw, typically located closest to the engine and away from the air filter, is the focus of fine adjustment. Listen carefully to the engine's rhythm as you tweak the screw, aiming for the highest idle RPM where the engine runs smoothly without engaging the chain. Once you reach this peak, gently turn the screw counterclockwise until the RPMs slightly decrease, marking the ideal idle setting.

If your chainsaw lacks clear labeling, remember that the low-speed screw is nearest to the engine. Begin adjusting, noting that turning the screw in will decrease RPMs. If turned too far, the RPMs will drop significantly. Conversely, turning it out will increase the RPMs until they peak and then start to fall again. Find the midpoint between these fluctuations - this is the optimal idling speed. From this point, gradually adjust the screw outwards until the RPMs just begin to decrease, then set it

For chainsaws experiencing persistent idling issues or lacking responsiveness, removing the limiter cap on the low-speed screw may be necessary for a wider adjustment range. If adjustments do not yield the expected results, consult online resources for guidance on removing the limiter cap specific to your chainsaw model and retry the tuning process. If problems persist, it may indicate a deeper issue with the chainsaw, requiring further investigation or professional servicing.

Fine-Tuning the High-Speed Screw

Adjusting the high-speed screw on a chainsaw is a delicate process critical for controlling the maximum RPMs. This procedure, although seemingly simple, holds the engine's integrity in the balance. Improper tuning of the high-speed screw can lead to over-revving, risking severe engine damage.

For precision in this task, a digital tachometer is invaluable. This device provides precise RPM measurements without requiring a direct engine connection. Simply hold it near the spark plug to obtain accurate readings on its digital display, ensuring you are informed about the engine's speed in real-time.

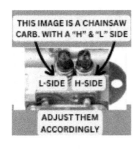

The role of the high-speed screw is to regulate the chainsaw's top speed. When the throttle is fully engaged, adjustments to the screw can either increase or decrease the engine's RPMs. Tightening the screw increases the speed, while loosening it reduces the pace. However, excessive tightening can push the engine beyond safe operational limits, potentially causing catastrophic failure.

If your chainsaw model includes a limiter cap, it is advisable to adhere to its preset limits. The limiter cap is designed to prevent over-tightening, safeguarding the engine from reaching dangerous speeds. If your chainsaw does not have this feature, consult online resources for the recommended initial high-speed screw settings specific to your model. These factory settings are carefully determined to prevent over-revving, providing a safe baseline

Chapter 9: Starter Handle, Cord and Recoil

Where the rope enters the recoil starter cover hole there is a metal bushing that wears out. It protects the plastic cover against the friction of the rope and is replaceable. It may wear to a sharp edge that damages the rope. Fully extend the rope and inspect it closest to the saw for fraying.

To replace a cord, you first feed it through the bushing and then into the hole in the recoil pulley. When it exits in the center pull it out and tie a knot close to the end of the rope. Pull the rope out so it seats in the notched area.

Now, wind the pulley against the spring in the direction you will pull it with the rope. When you reach the point where the spring stops you, you let the pulley go back one full turn. Then you thread the rope around the pulley and pull it tight. Feel the spring with your hand by twisting the pulley more. The spring must not bottom out. Slowly let the rope in under spring tension.

Chain Oil Tank, Pump and Hole

- Check the bar and chain oil level often. I suggest that you do this before each use. The design of many chainsaws will require that you top up the chain oil when refueling. Always check the oil level and refill.

- Clean out the chain-oil portal when maintaining the guide bar. Sawdust can block delivery of oil to the cutting chain.

- Use the correct grade and type of chain saw oil.

- We recommend that you use special chain oil with good adhesion characteristics as recommended by the manufacturer.

- Never use waste oil to lubricate the chain, it will cause damage to the oil pump, the bar and the chain.

- It is important to use oil of the correct viscosity range to suit the air temperature. In temperatures below 32°F some oils become too viscous, and can overload the oil pump. This will damage the oil pump components.

- A neglected chainsaw may have badly blocked oil channels that stops oil flow to the bar. As an alternative to stripping the oil pump, you could drain the oil from the oil tank and fill the tank with mineral spirits. Replace the cap to seal the tank and run the engine at low revolutions. It may take a while for the mineral spirits to wash out the old oil and clean the channels. Do not use gasoline, it dissolves all oil and leaves the pump too dry.

Replacing the Bar Tip Sprocket

You need not replace the bar for a worn or damaged bar-tip sprocket. You can replace the bar-tip instead. To do that, support the bar on wood with a hole under the bar-tip rivet. Punch the rivet with a center punch and drill it out with a drill that's slightly smaller than the shank of a new rivet. Remove the drill immediately when the rivet head becomes loose. Make sure the rivet is centered over the hole in the wood support and punch it out. Replace the bar-tip with a new one and peen the new rivet in place.

Replacing the drive sprocket

Replace a worn or damaged drive sprocket before it damages the chain. To get to the clutch mechanism you need to remove the bar and chain. Then you can remove the drive clutch. You will find more than one type of clutch in different chainsaws. On some you will see only the outside drum and the sprocket. To see the inside you have to remove it. Another type is the other way around and you can see the center shaft and inner clutch disk when you remove the bar.

Chainsaws have a centrifugal clutch inside a drum that expands as the engine speed increases. The clutch pawls contact the inside of the drum and drive it. fitted to the drum is a fixed spur sprocket, or a replaceable rim sprocket.

- The centrifugal mechanism of an inboard clutch is close to the chainsaw body. The drum, sprocket, and chain are on the outside, over the clutch, protecting the clutch mechanism. It is easy to replace the sprocket of an inboard clutch; especially when it is a rim sprocket. You remove the clutch side cover and pry off a circlip. You will also do this during routine maintenance to get to the clutch mechanism.
- The sprocket and the chain of an outboard clutch are behind the clutch

drum, close to the chainsaw body. The clutch mechanism fits inside the drum, visible from the outside. Changing the sprocket is a slower process on this clutch. To change the sprocket of an outboard clutch, remove the clutch and the drum, sometimes with a special tool. You also have to remove the spark plug and block off the piston so you can twist off the clutch.

The advantages of the outboard clutch are that it more rapidly and efficiently clears chips from behind the clutch cover. Both versions have a needle bearing on the drive shaft. You must grease the bearing with high quality bearing grease or engine oil at least once a week. If you use the chainsaw seasonally, check it before you use the chainsaw.

In your user manual you will find clear instructions to remove and service the clutch.

Throttle Trigger or Lockout

Throttle triggers on some models break, and then you will have to replace it. Do not operate a chainsaw with a damaged or malfunctioning trigger or lockout. Be sure that the saw chain stops moving when you release the throttle control trigger. How triggers work differs a lot, and getting to them for repairs, even more. It's almost like no two models are the same, and no manuals show the procedure. I found lots of YouTube videos for a specific make and model, some good, some bad. On some models it is straightforward and the parts are freely available. Costs are low if you do it yourself. If you cannot find the information, it will compel you to ask a dealer how.

Muffler and Spark Arrestor Screen

The purpose of the muffler is to reduce the noise level. It also directs the hot exhaust gasses away from the operator. The muffler vibrates a lot and may work loose, check it regularly to ensure it is secure.

The exhaust gasses can contain sparks and regulations may require a spark arrestor to prevent fires. If the manufacturer installed a spark arrestor screen in your muffler, clean it at least once a week with a wire brush.

Do not neglect the muffler and the screen, a muffler in poor condition will cause the engine to overheat, lose power, and may lead to serious damage. Replace a damaged screen, do not remove it, and do not puncture it to improve performance, you will gain nothing.

Spark Plug

The spark plug works in the heat of things. It wears out and you must attend to it to ensure maximum performance. It deteriorates from normal use and it's adversely affected by:

- A fuel mixture with an incorrect amount of oil, or even the wrong type, that causes a carbon build-up on the spark plug.
- A dirty air filter enriches the mixture on models that do not have computerized carburetors and causes deposits on the spark plug electrodes.

These conditions may cause power loss, hesitant acceleration and starting difficulties, and the chainsaw may run poorly at idle speed. I recommend that you always check the spark plug first before making any adjustments. Clean it if coated with black deposits or oil and set the electrode gap, usually 0.020 inch, but rather look it up in your manual. A spark plug in good condition is coated with light brown deposits, and the gap is correct.

Major manufacturers recommend replacing the spark plug after 100 operating hours. That's 20 five-hour workdays. It is a bad idea to replace the spark plug with another type; I recommend that you always use the recommended type. A spark plug that's too long will damage the piston and one that's too short will foul up.

How to Store a Chainsaw

Most manufacturers recommend draining the fuel and bar oil when readying the chainsaw for the winter. First you decant all the fuel and chain oil into clean containers and then you run the engine till it stops. It will clear out any fuel in the fuel lines and carburetor. After that you use a clean rag to clean the fuel and oil tanks. Service and clean the chainsaw and store it in a dry, clean environment.

Some users use fuel stabilizers and do not drain the fuel system. They say they can store the chainsaw for 6 months with no problems. It is not what the manufacturers recommend though, but, they also do not recommend using ethanol fuel. I believe it is best to use a fuel stabilizer with ethanol fuels anyway and I still recommend draining the fuel.

When Should You Take it Into an Authorized Service Center?

- When it stops working, the plug is good, the fuel, and the fuel lines are good. It refuses to start, whatever you try.

- When the operator's manual does not describe the required repairs, you search the internet and you do not feel comfortable with the recommendations.
- All manufacturers recommend that you take your chainsaw to a service center periodically for a major check-up. It depends on how often you use it and its condition but at least once in two years.
- When the service guy you phoned says you should bring it in for repairs.
- When the chainsaw is not as good as it used to be but you see nothing wrong, take it to the experts.

The Chain

Ensuring that your chainsaw's chain is kept sharp is a fundamental aspect of maintaining your chainsaw effectively. A sharp chain not only enhances the safety of your cutting operations but also improves the overall efficiency and performance of your equipment. The popular adage "a sharp chain is a safe chain" underscores the importance of maintaining the sharpness of your chainsaw's chain.

When the chain on your chainsaw is not adequately sharpened, you may find yourself exerting more physical effort to complete a cut. This can lead to accidents, as using excessive force can compromise your control over the chainsaw and increase the risk of injury. In contrast, a sharp chain enables smoother and easier cutting, reducing the strain on both the operator and the equipment.

Recognizing the signs that indicate the need for sharpening your chainsaw's chain is crucial for safe operation. If you encounter resistance while cutting through material or feel the chain "rocking," it is a clear indication that the chain requires sharpening. Taking breaks during your cutting tasks also presents an opportune moment to inspect and sharpen the chain, ensuring that your chainsaw operates at its optimal performance level.

Prior to sharpening the chain, it is essential to wear appropriate safety gear, such as gloves and safety glasses, to protect yourself from potential injuries. Allowing the chain to cool down before sharpening is recommended to prevent damage and ensure that the chain returns to its original specifications.

The process of sharpening your chainsaw's chain involves focusing on the most damaged cutter first and then adjusting the remaining teeth to match. While this process may be time-consuming, it is essential for achieving straight and effortless cuts once the sharpening is completed. Starting at the "indicator link" can help maintain consistency in sharpening, enabling you to sharpen one side of the chain before moving to the opposite side.

By following these guidelines and prioritizing the maintenance of your chainsaw's chain, you can ensure safe and efficient cutting operations while prolonging the lifespan of your equipment. Regular sharpening and proper maintenance of your chainsaw's chain are key practices that every chainsaw operator should prioritize for optimal performance and safety.

The ideal angles for sharpening the edges and gaps of your cutters are typically 30 degrees horizontally and 10 degrees vertically. It takes practice to develop a sense for this, so new sawyers are advised to use a round file guide when sharpening their chains. Chains often have guide marks on the top plate of the cutters to help with the correct left and right angles during sharpening. When using a round file, it is important to sharpen by sliding it from the tip to the base of the cutter. Avoid moving the file back and forth while in contact with the cutter, and ensure that the file only touches the gap while sliding from tip to base.

Continuing with Chain Maintenance:

Ensure you have the correct diameter round file for the gullets (the cutting surfaces of the teeth) of your specific chain, especially if you use chains of varying sizes. Using round files that are either too thick or too thin can result in undesirable filing of the gullets. Aim to use the same number of file strokes for each cutter, although some sawyers may need to add extra strokes for teeth that require the use of their non-dominant hand to compensate for reduced strength and coordination.

Use a raker guide to determine when to file down the rakers using a flat or bastard file. Only file them as much as needed to bring them level with the raker guide. Rakers typically need filing down only once every few cutting sessions. Just like round files, flat and bastard files should be used in a tip-to-base direction.

Ensure the drive links are in good condition without being excessively worn down. Occasionally, you may need to lightly file away curled edges, although this should not happen frequently. After maintaining the chain and bar, reinstall them onto the powerhead and adjust the tension. Proper tensioning means the chain has no sag but can still rotate easily when gripped between your thumb and index finger (with gloves on). The chain should also snap back into place when pulled away from the bottom of the bar. This skill improves with practice.

Before tensioning the chain, ensure it is facing the correct way when placed back on the bar and powerhead sprocket. One way to remember the correct orientation is to ensure "Santa's sleigh" is pointing toward the bar's tip. By looking closely at the raker and cutter, you may notice a resemblance to a sleigh, with the sleigh facing the bar's nose. It's important to avoid the embarrassment of tensioning the chain, starting the saw, and realizing you had the chain facing the wrong direction while trying to cut through wood. When conducting

In This Image, what to inspect before using your chainsaw:
1. Check the chain and bar – sharpness of chain, bar seated correctly.
2. Check the bolts and screws all around the saw – no missing screws or bolts.
3. Check the casing of the saw – no cracked or missing plastic.
4. Felling axe and wedges in good condition.

a thorough inspection in the vicinity of the powerhead of your chainsaw, it is essential to pay close attention to various key components to ensure optimal performance and safety during operation.

Firstly, take a moment to scan the area for any sizable pieces of woody debris that may obstruct the smooth rotation of the flywheel when starting the chainsaw. It is crucial to remove any such

The Throttle is Where the Two Black Arrows are Pointing To

obstacles to prevent any hindrance to the pull cord during startup operations.

Next, carefully examine the functionality of the on/off choke switch, throttle trigger, and throttle interlock controls. Ensure that these controls can be manipulated effortlessly without encountering any resistance caused by dust or debris. Any grittiness in the controls could lead to them locking up at an inopportune moment, potentially compromising the safe operation of the chainsaw.

Moreover, verify that the throttle can only be engaged after the throttle interlock is depressed. This safety feature is designed to prevent the accidental engagement of the throttle before the interlock is properly activated. By adhering to this sequence, you can minimize the risk of unintended throttle acceleration, enhancing overall safety during operation.

Furthermore, it is crucial to inspect and tighten all screws around the powerhead, including those securing the muffler. Loose muffler screws can result in a metallic rattling sound while the chainsaw is in use, which may indicate potential issues that need to be addressed promptly to maintain optimal performance.

Additionally, pay attention to the condition of the spark arrestor and ensure that it is not clogged. If blockages are present, carefully remove and clean the spark arrestor using a toothbrush and a small amount of fuel to disintegrate any exhaust residue. Reinstall the spark arrestor once it has been thoroughly cleaned to maintain proper functionality. While some individuals may consider removing the spark arrestor to improve the chainsaw's performance, it is important to note that doing so is illegal in most areas due to the increased risk of starting wildfires. Keeping the spark arrestor clean and properly installed is essential for both performance and safety.

Fuel:

When fueling your chainsaw, it is essential to ensure that the gasoline meets three critical criteria: high octane, ethanol-free, and mixed with two-cycle engine oil. These factors are vital for the optimal performance and longevity of your chainsaw's engine. The recommended fuel mixture ratio is 50:1, which means you should mix 50 parts of gasoline with 1 part of two-cycle engine oil.

To simplify this, remember that for every 1 gallon of gasoline, you need to add 2.5 ounces of two-cycle engine oil. This ratio is crucial because it ensures that the engine receives adequate lubrication, which helps in maintaining the efficiency and durability of the chainsaw's moving parts. Inadequate lubrication can lead to increased friction, overheating, and potential engine seizure. Many lawn and garden retailers conveniently sell two-cycle engine oil in 2.5-ounce and 5-ounce containers, making it easy to measure and mix the correct amounts without the need for additional measuring tools. This convenience helps ensure that you consistently achieve the precise 50:1 fuel mixture ratio required for your chainsaw.

It's a good practice to mark your fuel container with the date it was filled and the mixture ratio. This labeling helps you keep track of the freshness of the fuel and prevents any mix-up that could result in using the wrong fuel in your chainsaw or other equipment. Using the incorrect fuel mixture in a four-cycle engine, for instance, can cause significant damage, just as using pure gasoline in a two-cycle engine like your chainsaw can lead to severe operational issues.

Before pouring the fuel mixture into your chainsaw, it is crucial to shake the fuel container vigorously for several seconds. This action ensures that the gasoline and engine oil are thoroughly mixed. Over time, the oil can separate from the gasoline, leading to an uneven mixture. If you pour improperly mixed fuel into your chainsaw, the piston and other internal components might not receive the necessary lubrication, increasing the risk of engine damage or seizure.

In summary, paying close attention to the quality of the gasoline, maintaining the correct fuel-to-oil ratio, and ensuring thorough mixing before each use are essential steps in keeping your chainsaw running smoothly and efficiently. Proper fuel management helps extend the life of your chainsaw, enhances its performance, and reduces the likelihood of costly repairs. Inspect the lever/hand guard for any signs of damage, ensuring that it is not cracked or compromised in any way. Verify that the hinge pivots smoothly without any gritty sensations, and that the lever provides a distinct click when engaging or disengaging the chain brake. The chain brake is a critical safety feature, and any concerns regarding its integrity should be addressed before using the chainsaw to ensure safe operation.

Lastly, check that the dogs are securely fastened to the cover plate and powerhead. These components play a vital role in providing stability while cutting, so it is important to ensure they are snug and unable to shift during operation, as any movement could pose a safety hazard. By meticulously examining these key elements around the powerhead of your chainsaw, you can enhance both performance and safety while using this powerful tool.

In layman's terms, another way to explain gasoline to two-cycle engine oil and the ratios is:

When selecting fuel for your chainsaw, focus on three key aspects: high octane content, absence of ethanol, and proper mixing with two-cycle engine oil. The ideal fuel mixture ratio is 50:1 - that's 50 parts gasoline to 1 part oil. For easy mixing, use 2.5 ounces of two-cycle oil per gallon of gas. Many garden stores sell pre-measured oil containers, simplifying the process.

Label your fuel container with the mixing date and ratio to avoid confusion with other engine types. Before refueling your chainsaw, shake

the container thoroughly to ensure proper
mixing of gas and oil. This step is crucial for
proper engine lubrication and to prevent engine
seizure.

THIS IMAGE IS A
GASOLINE/OIL MIXTURES

VERY HELPFUL GUIDE

Continuing with Fluids:

Before removing the cap,
clean any debris around it
to prevent dirt from
entering the fuel reservoir and fuel filter. Avoid
opening the bar oil reservoir while the fuel
reservoir is open to prevent spillage if the
chainsaw is accidentally tipped over. It also
helps you keep track of which reservoir has
been filled. Ensure you wear safety glasses
before unscrewing the fuel cap, as gasoline
can be highly volatile under pressure from the
chainsaw's hot temperature. If the cap is
difficult to remove due to pressure, let the
chainsaw cool in a shaded area before trying
again. Use a funnel to avoid spills, as spilled oil

can attract dust on the saw's surface. Avoid overfilling the reservoir to prevent spillage when closing the cap. Always secure the cap fully after refilling, looking for a snap or click indicating it's properly closed. Ideally, you should run out of fuel before bar oil to prevent damage to the bar and chain from overheating, stretching, and warping.

In the section discussing fluids and fuel maintenance, it is advised to wear safety glasses when checking the fuel filter by removing the fuel cap. During inspection, focus on looking for physical damage and any discoloration in the fuel filter and its hose. Check the hose for cracks or tears, and replace it if any damage is found, although replacing it may require disassembling the fueling system. Similarly, inspect the fuel filter for cracks or tears, and replace it if necessary. Also, pay attention to the color of the fuel filter; if it appears gray or off-white, it's recommended to replace it to prevent future fueling issues, even if the chainsaw has been running well. Learning to identify the subtle color changes in the filter takes practice but becomes easier with experience.

Fuel hose length can be a challenge when replacing chainsaw fuel filters. A clean pair of improvised chopsticks can help fish out the filter from the fuel tank. Use one hand to manipulate the chopsticks and hold the fuel hose near the tank opening, while using the other to insert the new filter.

When handling fuel and oil reservoirs, follow these precautions:

1. Clean debris from caps before opening.

2. Open only one reservoir at a time to prevent spills and track refills.

3. Wear safety glasses when refilling, even for bar oil.

Bar oil is specially formulated for chainsaw lubrication and should not be substituted. Use a funnel when refilling, especially for bar oil, to avoid spills near the muffler and cooling fins.

Don't overfill reservoirs, and ensure caps are securely fastened.

For field work, combination canisters (also called combi fuel cans or dolmars) are ideal for transporting fuel mixture and bar oil. These typically hold enough for two refills of standard chainsaws before needing a refill themselves. Regrettably, fuel hoses are often too short, which can make replacing the fuel filter a challenging task for many chainsaw users. To address this common issue, a helpful recommendation is to utilize clean chopsticks as makeshift tools to reach into the fuel reservoir and assist in bringing the fuel filter to the surface for replacement. By using one hand to hold the fuel hose near the reservoir opening with the help of chopsticks, and the other hand to carefully insert the new fuel filter, the process can be made more manageable and efficient.

Before proceeding to open the fuel reservoir cap for maintenance, it is crucial to ensure that any debris or dirt is wiped away from the cap area. This preventive measure helps in avoiding contamination of the bar oil reservoir, which can lead to potential issues with the chainsaw's performance. Additionally, it is essential not to open the bar oil reservoir while the fuel reservoir is also open. This precautionary step not only prevents accidental spillage of fluids in case of a mishap but also aids in keeping track of which reservoir has been refilled and which still requires attention. When dealing with bar oil, a safety precaution to keep in mind is to wear protective glasses to shield your eyes from any potential splashes or spills. Bar oil, being a specialized lubricant designed specifically for chainsaw bars and chains, requires careful handling during refilling. Using a funnel during the refilling process is recommended, particularly for bar oil due to its sticky nature. Overfilling the reservoir should be avoided to prevent spillage when re-securing the cap after refilling. It is crucial to ensure that the cap is tightly secured to prevent any leaks or contamination.

For those who require a convenient solution for transporting fuel and bar oil on a job site, a combination canister proves to be a practical and efficient choice. These versatile canisters, known by various names such as combi fuel cans or dolmars in the wildland firefighting community, offer ample storage capacity for fuel mixture and bar oil. With the ability to refill most chainsaws twice before needing a refill themselves, these canisters provide a reliable and portable solution for chainsaw users who need to work on multiple tasks without interruptions.

In an ideal scenario, when your chainsaw is finely tuned, you can expect the levels of fuel and oil in its reservoirs to diminish at similar rates. This equilibrium is maintained by the design of the combined canister, where both compartments are intended to deplete at corresponding rates. The volumes of these compartments are meticulously crafted to mirror the proportions of the fuel and bar reservoirs in your chainsaw.

To simplify the process of refilling the combined canister, it is helpful to remember that the smaller compartment is designated for bar oil. This aligns with the setup of the chainsaw, where the bar oil reservoir is typically smaller than the fuel reservoir. Conversely, the larger compartment in the combined canister is specifically tailored to complement the larger fuel reservoir of the chainsaw.

By understanding these proportional relationships and design principles, you can ensure that your chainsaw operates efficiently and effectively. Monitoring and maintaining the fluid levels in both the individual reservoirs and the combined canister will contribute to the optimal performance and longevity of your chainsaw.

If your chainsaw is working right, you'll notice something cool: the gas and oil should run out at about the same time. It's pretty handy, actually. And get this – those combo cans you use to refill? They're designed to match up with your saw perfectly.

The trick is to remember that the smaller part of the can is for the bar oil, just like how the oil tank on your saw is the smaller one. The bigger section? That's for your fuel mix. It all lines up nicely with how your chainsaw is built. So when you're running low, you can just grab that combo can and fill 'er up without having to think too much about it. Pretty clever design, if you ask me. Makes life a bit easier when you're out there working with your saw.

"Mastering the Fluid Dance: Your Chainsaw's Secret Rhythm"

Picture this: your chainsaw isn't just a tool; it's a finely tuned instrument performing a delicate ballet of fuel and oil. When you've got it dialed in just right, something magical happens – the fuel and oil reservoirs empty in perfect harmony. It's like they're dancing to the same beat, and let me tell you, that's when your saw really sings.

Now, here's where it gets interesting. Those combo canisters you use for refills? They're not just convenient; they're engineering marvels. They're designed to mirror your saw's thirst, with compartments sized to match your chainsaw's tanks. It's like they've got ESP or something.

Here's a pro tip that'll make you feel like a chainsaw whisperer: the smaller compartment in your combo can is for bar oil. Why? Because your saw's bar oil tank is the petite one. The bigger section? That's your fuel mix's home away from home. It's not rocket science, but knowing this little secret will make you look like a seasoned pro at the worksite.

But wait, there's more! This isn't just about convenience; it's about peak performance. By keeping these fluid levels in check and using this matched refill system, you're not just fueling your saw – you're unleashing its full potential. You're giving it exactly what it needs to tackle any job with gusto.

So next time you're out there, listen closely. You might just hear your chainsaw humming a little tune of appreciation as you fill it up with precision. And who knows? With this knowledge in your back pocket, you might find yourself becoming the go-to guru for all things chainsaw in your circle.

Remember, it's not just about cutting wood – it's about cutting wood with style, efficiency, and a deep understanding of your tool's innermost workings. Now that's what I call sawing with swagger! So let's do this!

Here's a simpler version of the instructions for preparing your chainsaw before fieldwork:

Getting Your Chainsaw Ready for the Field

Before you head out to your cutting site, it's crucial to check if your chainsaw starts properly. This saves you from a frustrating situation where you hike a long way only to find your saw won't work.

Safety First:

1. Wear your protective gear (PPE).

2. Keep others at a safe distance to protect their hearing.

3. Engage the chain brake.

Two Ways to Start the Saw Safely:

1. Ground Start:

    - Step on the rear handle with your right foot.

    - Hold the front handle with your left hand.

    - Pull the starter cord with your right hand.

2. Between-Legs Start:

    - Grip the saw between your legs.

    - Hold the front handle with your left hand.

    - Pull the starter cord with your right hand.

Important: Always use your right hand to pull the starter cord. Never try to "drop start" the saw - it's dangerous and gives you less control. By following these steps, you'll ensure your chainsaw is ready for work and you're using it safely. Would you like me to explain any part of this in more detail?

Before starting the chainsaw

It is crucial to ensure the safety of your teammates and any bystanders in the vicinity. This can be achieved by clearly and loudly announcing your intention to start the saw, giving everyone a chance to move to a safe distance and avoid any potential hazards.

To prepare the saw for starting, begin by priming it in the full choke position. Typically, it only takes 1-4 pulls to prime the engine and get it ready for ignition. If the saw does not prime after a few attempts, adjust the mixture control lever to half choke and continue pulling the starter cord until the engine "burps" and primes successfully, which usually happens within a few pulls.

In the event that the saw still does not prime, move the control lever to the run position and try starting the saw again. With the proper priming and setting, the saw should start within a couple of pulls, avoiding unnecessary strain on the engine.

It is important to note that attempting to start the saw in the same position after it has primed without adjusting the mixture control lever can lead to flooding, where an excess of fuel accumulates in the carburetor and combustion chamber. If flooding occurs, it is best to set the chainsaw aside and allow the excess fuel to evaporate naturally from the combustion chamber.

To accelerate the evaporation process, you can remove the spark plug and gently pull the starter cord. The hissing sound you hear indicates that the piston is pushing out both air and excess fuel from the chamber. By repeating this process a few times, you can effectively clear the chamber of any flooded fuel, ensuring a smooth and safe start-up when you next attempt to use the chainsaw.

Before starting the chainsaw, loudly declare your intent to operate it. This alerts nearby team members and onlookers to maintain a safe distance, especially in confined spaces.

Begin with the saw in full choke position. Pull the starter cord 1-4 times to "burp" the engine. If unsuccessful, move the mixture control to half choke and attempt to start again, still aiming for 1-4 pulls. If it doesn't start, switch to the run position and try once more. The saw should start within a couple of pulls if it hasn't already.

Caution:

Continuing to pull the cord without adjusting the mixture control after a burp can flood the saw. This occurs when excess fuel in the carburetor and combustion chamber prevents ignition. To fix this, allow the saw to sit until the fuel evaporates, or speed up the process by removing the spark plug and slowly pulling the cord several times. Listen for a hissing sound, indicating that air and vaporized fuel are being expelled from the chamber.

Chainsaws with larger engine displacements often present a challenge when it comes to starting them up. The high compression in the combustion chamber can make it tough to smoothly pull the starting cord. This difficulty can sometimes lead to the cord abruptly extending out and stopping suddenly, creating a jarring experience for the user. To address this issue, many larger chainsaws are equipped with a decompression valve located on the top of the powerhead.

By depressing the decompression valve, a small airway opens up, leading to the combustion chamber. This action helps to release some of the excessive pressure, making it easier to start the chainsaw. It's important to depress the valve each time you attempt to start the chainsaw, as the pressure generated during each start-up attempt can push the valve back outward.

If your chainsaw is already warmed up, a useful technique is to lightly press the throttle while keeping the chain brake engaged. This action will slightly rev the engine and bring the idle down to lower RPMs, preventing the clutch from expanding too much and engaging the drum, which could result in smoking. It's advisable not to hold in the throttle for an extended period to bring the idle down, as this could cause the clutch to engage the drum unnecessarily while the chain brake is engaged. A quick bump of the throttle is all that is needed in this situation.

On the other hand, if your chainsaw is not yet warmed up, it's essential to ensure that the powerhead reaches the optimal operating temperature before attempting to cut through any wood. To achieve this, simply rev the engine up and down until you no longer see exhaust fumes. This process ensures that the engine is sufficiently warmed up and ready for cutting tasks.

Some larger chainsaws can be challenging to start due to high compression in the combustion chamber. This can make pulling the starter cord difficult or cause it to stop abruptly. Many of these saws feature a decompression valve on the powerhead. Pressing this valve creates a small air passage to the combustion chamber, reducing excessive pressure and making it easier to pull the cord.

Press the valve before each start attempt, as the pressure from each try will push the valve back out.

For a warm saw, lightly tap the throttle while the chain brake is on. This briefly revs the engine and lowers the idle RPM. This step is crucial because high idle speeds can cause the clutch to expand, engaging the drum and potentially causing smoke. Avoid holding the throttle down, as this can unnecessarily engage the clutch and drum while the brake is on. A quick tap is sufficient.

If the saw is cold, warm up the powerhead before cutting. Do this by revving the engine up and down until you no longer see exhaust fumes.

When testing the bar oiling settings of your chainsaw, it's important to ensure that the bar and chain are properly lubricated before starting cutting operations. To do this, start the chainsaw and bring the chain up to cutting speeds. Hold the tip of the bar close to a piece of wood (avoid rocks) without actually cutting it, and check if you can see a visible oil line being applied onto the wood. It's better for the chainsaw to have excess oil (even "vomit" oil) and require more frequent refills than to risk inadequate lubrication by conserving the bar oil.

You can adjust the oiler settings using a turn dial located on the powerhead. Turn the dial up gradually until you can see the oil lines being applied without difficulty in confirming their presence. Additionally, it's recommended to keep extra parts and specific quantities in your dedicated tool kit for trimming tasks.

The following parts are essential for ensuring uninterrupted chainsaw operation throughout a full day of cutting:

1. E-clips
2. Washers (2 should suffice)
3. Drive sprocket (1)
4. Clutch drum (1)
5. Needle bearings (2)
6. Fuel filters (2)
7. Air filter (1)
8. Spark plugs (2)
9. Spark arrestor (1)
10. Body screws (3 should be adequate)
11. Bar nuts (2, assuming they are not "captured")
12. Chains (minimum of 2)
13. Scrench (1) - It's crucial to keep this versatile tool handy to avoid any troubleshooting issues during cutting tasks. Furthermore, having a complete set of personal protective equipment (PPE) is highly

recommended if budget allows. At a minimum, ensure you have an extra pair of safety glasses and earplugs available to protect your eyes and ears, which are invaluable assets for your overall well-being. Invest in quality equipment to safeguard these vital sensory organs as you navigate through your cutting activities. Merely relying on a single trimming tool and a handful of extra parts will prove insufficient when tackling extensive cutting tasks. To effectively handle the demands of large-scale cutting projects, it is essential to equip yourself with a comprehensive array of accessories. In fact, a well-rounded toolkit comprising various essential items is crucial to ensure a safe and productive day of cutting in the field.

Here is a detailed list of items that I recommend including in your complete trimming tool field kit:

1. A durable scabbard specifically designed for the bar and chain, with a preference for a

full-coverage case to provide optimal protection and safety during transportation and storage.

2. Ensure you have a full combination canister at your disposal to conveniently store and carry essential liquids and fuels required for operating your trimming tool.

3. It is advisable to have at least one fluid funnel in your kit, with two being preferred to have dedicated funnels for fuel and bar oil, respectively.

4. Keep a supply of rags handy for wiping off any spills or messes that may occur during cutting operations to maintain a clean and safe working environment.

5. Include a felling axe in your toolkit to assist in cutting and manipulating trees and branches effectively.

6. Have an assortment of wedges available to aid in tree felling and prevent dangerous situations such as pinching the saw blade.

7. A reliable hand saw should also be included in your kit as a versatile cutting tool for various tasks that may require more precision.

8. Consider adding loppers to your kit as an optional tool for cutting smaller branches and limbs with ease.

9. Equip yourself with a length of strong rope to safely manage and pull down any hang-ups or entangled branches during cutting operations.

10. Ensure you have a selection of round files in varying diameters to match your chain specifications, storing them individually in plastic straws to reduce frictional wear and maintain their sharpness.

11. Invest in a round file guide, especially if you are new to using a chainsaw and require assistance in sharpening the chain effectively.

12. Include a raker guide in your kit to help maintain the proper depth and angle of the rakers on your chain for optimal cutting performance.

13. Have a flat or bastard file on hand to address any nicks or curled edges on the chain, ensuring smooth and efficient cutting.

14. Consider adding a bar file to your kit as an optional tool for refining the bar's edges, or use the flat or bastard file for this purpose if needed.

15. Make sure to have a screwdriver, preferably with a Torx bit, for adjusting and maintaining the body screws of your trimming tool.

16. Keep a toothbrush in your kit for cleaning and maintaining hard-to-reach areas of your equipment, ensuring smooth operation and longevity.

17. Don't forget to include bearing grease in your kit to lubricate moving parts and extend the lifespan of your equipment.

18. Consider adding a nose sprocket greasing device to your kit as an optional tool for ensuring smooth operation and longevity of the nose sprocket.

By incorporating these recommended items into your chainsaw tool field kit, you can enhance your efficiency, safety, and overall cutting performance when taking on large-scale cutting tasks.

First and foremost, the primary goal of every individual engaged in chainsaw operations is to ensure personal safety and well-being. It is crucial to prioritize returning home at the end of each day with all limbs, fingers, and senses intact. To achieve this goal, it is essential to take meticulous care in protecting oneself, colleagues, spectators, and property during all chainsaw-related activities.

Listed below are the recommended personal protective equipment (PPE) and safety items that should be worn and readily available for immediate access during chainsaw operations:

1. Helmet: Check the expiration date and ensure a snug fit to provide adequate head protection.

2. Safety glasses: Opt for impact-rated eyewear that meets ANSI Z87+ standards to safeguard the eyes from debris and potential hazards.

3. Hearing protection: Select high-quality ear protection that offers optimal defense against loud noises, ensuring comfort while wearing a helmet. Consider using a combination of earplugs and earmuffs for enhanced protection.

4. Long sleeve shirt: Choose a buttoned-up, well-fitted shirt to minimize exposure to chainsaw-related risks.

5. Brightly colored and reflective safety vest: Wear as required by organizational or local regulations to increase visibility and promote safety.

6. Leather gloves: Provide hand protection against cuts and abrasions while operating the chainsaw.

7. Long pants: Opt for durable, full-length pants to shield the legs from potential injuries.

8. Chainsaw chaps: Inspect for any signs of damage, ensuring they are free of nicks, missing internal layers, and large oil, fuel, or debris stains. Note that petroleum products can degrade the fibers of chainsaw chaps.

9. 8" boots: Lace up sturdy boots securely for stable footing, ensuring that the chaps overlap the boots by at least 2 inches.

10. Fire extinguisher with tourniquet and QuikClot: Keep these emergency tools readily accessible for immediate use in case of accidents or injuries.

11. First aid kit with tourniquet and QuikClot: Have a well-equipped first aid kit on hand to address any injuries promptly.

12. Cell phone and SPOT device: Carry a cell phone along with a long-range secondary communication device such as SPOT for emergency communication, particularly in remote locations.

13. Swamper: Assign a helper who can assist in various tasks, serve as a lookout, and provide aid during emergencies.

14. Remove loose clothing or jewelry before operating the chainsaw to prevent entanglement or accidents.

15. Remember to work at a controlled pace, as slow and steady movements are more effective than rushing through tasks. While speed may improve with practice, prioritizing safety and precision is paramount.

16. Respect your "blood bubble": Be mindful of the area around the chainsaw where potential harm can occur. Avoid allowing any objects or individuals into this zone that you are not prepared to eliminate.

By diligently following these safety guidelines and utilizing the recommended PPE and safety measures, individuals can significantly reduce the risk of accidents and injuries while operating a chainsaw. Prioritizing safety not only protects oneself but also ensures the well-being of others and the preservation of property during chainsaw operations.

Here are some detailed guidelines for operating trimmer tools, particularly chainsaws, to ensure safety and efficiency in your work:

1. Mental and Physical Preparedness: It is crucial to only operate a chainsaw when you are mentally and physically sharp. If you are feeling tired, distracted, or unwell, it is best to postpone using the chainsaw to prevent accidents and injuries.

2. Responsibility and Control: As the operator, you have the primary responsibility for everything that happens within your work area. While you can have assistance from lookouts, it is essential to maintain control over your work zone. Before making any cuts, communicate your actions, assess and mitigate potential hazards, and maintain a stable stance to facilitate quick escapes if needed.

3. Proper Handling Techniques: Avoid holding the chainsaw with your right hand while operating the throttle with your left hand, as this can hinder the activation of the chain brake lever in emergencies. Left-handed operators should adjust their technique to ensure safety and efficiency.

4. Avoiding Kickback Risks: Always stand to the side of your cutting line and refrain from standing directly behind or in line with the bar and chain of the saw to minimize the risk of kickback injuries. Keep your thumb wrapped around the handle at all times for better control and to ensure the chain brake engages automatically in case of kickback.

5. Body Positioning and Movement: Avoid going down on both knees while operating the chainsaw, as this can limit your ability to move quickly in response to falling or rolling materials. Onlookers should maintain a safe distance of at least two and a half lengths away

from the tree being cut to avoid potential hazards.

6. Ergonomic Stance and Resting Techniques: Maintain a relaxed stance while operating the chainsaw to prevent fatigue. Allow the saw to hang down the full length of your arms and consider resting the powerhead on one of your thighs when not actively cutting. Taking regular breaks for food and water is essential to sustain your energy levels and focus throughout your workday, similar to how you provide regular maintenance for your chainsaw to ensure its optimal performance and longevity.

The Conclusion

Conclusion: Proper chainsaw maintenance is essential, even though it requires a significant amount of effort. Investing time in servicing your saw will pay off immensely when it's time to use it. Neglecting maintenance during cutting sessions might save time initially, but you'll likely spend much more time later trying to restore the saw to proper working condition. Additionally, inadequate maintenance can lead to accelerated wear and damage to the saw parts and significantly increase the risk of injury to the operator and bystanders.

Chainsaws are powerful tools, and with that power comes the responsibility to maintain them correctly. Routine maintenance ensures that your chainsaw operates at peak efficiency, making your work easier and more effective. It's not just about keeping the chainsaw running; it's about ensuring that it runs safely and reliably. A well-maintained chainsaw provides smoother cuts, requires less effort to operate, and reduces the likelihood of unexpected breakdowns. Proper maintenance includes regular cleaning, checking and replacing the chain, ensuring that the bar is in good condition, and making sure that all moving parts are well-lubricated. Ignoring these tasks can lead to performance issues and potentially dangerous situations.

If you find yourself mentally or physically exhausted after completing the maintenance steps outlined earlier, don't hesitate to pack up your saw and take a break. The trees and brush will still be there for you to cut down another day. The potential loss of life or injury is not worth pushing yourself to reach a stopping point. It's okay to stop early, knowing you'll return home safely with all your limbs, digits, and senses intact. Your future self will appreciate the care you took to protect these vital assets.

Fatigue can impair your judgment and reaction times, increasing the risk of accidents. It's crucial to listen to your body and recognize when it's time to stop. Overexertion can lead to mistakes that could have severe consequences. Remember, no tree or brush pile is worth risking your health and safety. Taking regular breaks and ensuring you are well-rested before operating your chainsaw can prevent accidents and make your work more enjoyable and productive.

Ultimately, as the operator, you are responsible for the saw and everything within your area of influence. This means safeguarding yourself, your colleagues, bystanders, animals, pets, structures, other property, and your equipment. Never hesitate to refuse any task, request, or situation that makes you uncomfortable. Asking questions and double-checking your surroundings are always recommended and appreciated safety measures. When in doubt, there is no shame in turning down a job or task to ensure you live to see another day.

Chainsaw operation involves more than just physical skill; it requires constant awareness and vigilance. Always survey your work area for potential hazards, such as unstable trees, hidden obstacles, or dangerous weather conditions. Communicate clearly with anyone nearby and establish clear signals to indicate when the saw is in use. Personal protective equipment (PPE) such as gloves, eye protection, ear protection, and appropriate clothing should always be worn. These precautions are not just for your safety but for the safety of everyone around you.

With that said, there's only one thing left to do: get out there, service that chainsaw, and get to work! Ensuring your chainsaw is in top condition before you start your task will make your work smoother and safer. Remember, a well-maintained tool is a reliable partner in any cutting task. Take pride in your equipment and the work you do, knowing that you are taking all the necessary steps to protect yourself and those around you. Happy cutting!

Bonus 50 Multiple Choice Questions TO Test your Knowledge

1. Which of the following is a recommended safety item for chainsaw operations?

A) Sunglasses

B) Earplugs

C) Flip-flops

D) Tank tops

2. What should you check regarding your helmet before using it for chainsaw operations?

A) Expiration date

B) Color

C) Brand

D) Style

3. Which type of gloves are recommended for protecting hands during chainsaw operations?

A) Cotton gloves

B) Rubber gloves

C) Leather gloves

D) Wool gloves

4. What is the purpose of wearing a brightly colored and reflective safety vest during chainsaw operations?

A) To keep warm

B) To increase visibility

C) To store tools

D) To make a fashion statement

5. How should long pants be worn during chainsaw operations?

A) Rolled up

B) Tucked into socks

C) Short shorts

D) Full-length

6. What should you look for when inspecting chainsaw chaps?

A) Stains

B) Holes

C) Missing layers

D) All of the above

7. Why is it important for chainsaw chaps to overlap boots by at least 2 inches?

A) For fashion purposes

B) To protect the boots

C) To prevent debris from entering

D) To provide extra protection

8. Which of the following is an essential item to have for emergencies during chainsaw operations?

A) A map

B) A compass

C) A fire extinguisher

D) A blanket

9. What is the purpose of a tourniquet in the context of chainsaw operations?

A) To tie back hair

B) To secure loose clothing

C) To control bleeding

D) To measure tree diameter

10. What should a swamper do during chainsaw operations?

A) Perform solo tasks

B) Provide assistance

C) Wear bright clothing

D) Take breaks

11. Why is it important to remove jewelry before operating a chainsaw?

A) To avoid fashion clashes

B) To prevent accidents

C) To showcase bare hands

D) To improve visibility

12. How should one approach the speed of chainsaw operations?

A) Slow and steady

B) Fast and furious

C) Inconsistent pace

D) Rapid acceleration

13. What is the purpose of the "blood bubble" concept in chainsaw safety?

A) To mark cutting areas

B) To avoid distractions

C) To determine safe zones

D) To prevent injuries

14. Which item is recommended for communication in remote areas during chainsaw operations?

A) Walkie-talkie

B) Cell phone

C) Smoke signals

D) Telegram

15. Why is it important to prioritize safety over speed during chainsaw operations?

A) To finish quickly

B) To avoid accidents

C) To impress others

D) To save time

16. What is the primary goal of wearing safety glasses during chainsaw operations?

A) To improve vision

B) To look stylish

C) To protect eyes

D) To shield from rain

17. What should be the fit of a safety helmet for chainsaw operations?

A) Loose

B) Snug

C) Oversized

D) Backward

18. Why is it essential to have a first aid kit readily available during chainsaw operations?

A) For fashion emergencies

B) To fix broken tools

C) To address injuries

D) To store snacks

19. Which protective item is designed to shield legs from chainsaw-related injuries?

A) Arm warmers

B) Knee pads

C) Chainsaw chaps

D) Elbow guards

20. Why is it important to have a fire extinguisher on hand during chainsaw operations?

A) To keep warm

B) To put out fires

C) To cook food

D) To mark territory

21. What is the purpose of a swamper in the context of chainsaw operations?

A) To clean up debris

B) To rotate duties

C) To provide entertainment

D) To take photographs

22. How should long sleeve shirts be worn during chainsaw operations?

A) Backward

B) Inside out

C) Buttoned up

D) Tied around the waist

23. Which of the following is a recommended safety measure for chainsaw operations?

A) Listening to loud music

B) Rushing through cuts

C) Taking breaks frequently

D) Working at a controlled pace

24. Why is it important to have a cell phone and secondary communication device during chainsaw operations in remote areas?

A) To play games

B) To order food

C) For emergency communication

D) To take selfies

25. Which of the following items is NOT recommended for wearing during chainsaw operations?

A) Earmuffs

B) Tank tops

C) Leather gloves

D) Safety glasses

Here Are The Answers

1. B) Earplugs

2. A) Expiration date

3. C) Leather gloves

4. B) To increase visibility

5. D) Full-length

6. D) All of the above

7. D) To provide extra protection

8. C) A fire extinguisher

9. C) To control bleeding

10. B) Provide assistance

11. B) To prevent accidents

12. A) Slow and steady

13. D) To prevent injuries

14. B) Cell phone

15. B) To avoid accidents

16. C) To protect eyes

17. B) Snug

18. C) To address injuries

19. C) Chainsaw chaps

20. B) To put out fires

21. B) To rotate duties

22. C) Buttoned up

23. D) Working at a controlled pace

24. C) For emergency communication

25. B) Tank tops

Resources and Websites on 2-stroke and 4-stroke chainsaws:

Manufacturer Websites:

Stihl: The official Stihl website offers a comprehensive range of chainsaws, including both 2-stroke and 4-stroke models. You can find detailed specifications, features, and user manuals for their products.

Husqvarna:

Visit the official Husqvarna website to explore their lineup of chainsaws, including information about 2-stroke and 4-stroke options. You can also find maintenance tips and product registration information.

Echo:

The Echo USA website provides information on their chainsaw models, including 2-stroke and 4-stroke variants. You can access product manuals, warranty details, and explore their range of accessories.

Retailer Websites:

Home Depot:

Home Depot's website features a wide selection of chainsaws from various brands, allowing you to compare prices, read customer reviews, and make informed purchasing decisions.

Lowe's:

Lowe's online platform offers an assortment of chainsaw models, including both 2-stroke and 4-stroke options. You can check product availability, explore financing options, and find related accessories.

Amazon:

Amazon is a popular online marketplace where you can find a wide variety of chainsaws from different manufacturers. You can read customer reviews, compare prices, and benefit from fast shipping options.

Chainsaw Review Websites:

Chainsaw Journal:

Chainsaw Journal provides in-depth reviews, comparisons, and buying guides for a wide range of chainsaw models, including 2-stroke and 4-stroke options. You can access detailed product evaluations and expert recommendations.

Pro Tool Reviews:

Pro Tool Reviews offers professional reviews and insights on chainsaws, helping you make informed decisions when selecting a 2-stroke or 4-stroke chainsaw. You can find performance evaluations and industry trends on their website.

Popular Mechanics:

Popular Mechanics features articles and guides on outdoor power equipment, including chainsaws. You can explore their recommendations for 2-stroke and 4-stroke chainsaws and learn about maintenance tips.

Chainsaw Forums:

Arboristsite.com:

Arboristsite.com is a popular online forum where chainsaw enthusiasts and professionals discuss various topics related to chainsaws, including 2-stroke and 4-stroke models. You can ask questions, share experiences, and seek advice from the community.

Chainsaw Repair Forum:

Chainsaw Repair Forum is a resource for chainsaw owners looking for troubleshooting tips, repair advice, and maintenance guides. You can find discussions on different chainsaw brands and models, including 2-stroke and 4-stroke variants.

YouTube Channels:

- **Wranglerstar:** Wranglerstar's YouTube channel features reviews, demonstrations, and tutorials on chainsaws and outdoor equipment. You can watch videos on 2-stroke and 4-stroke chainsaws, learn about proper usage, and maintenance tips.

Project Farm:

Project Farm conducts thorough testing and comparison videos on various tools, including chainsaws. You can watch their reviews of 2-stroke and 4-stroke chainsaws to help you make an informed purchasing decision.

WWW.FAMILYHANDYMAN.COM

WWW.KHOW.COM

WWW.FORESTRY.COM

WWW.STIHLUSA.COM

WWW.HUSQVARNA.COM

WWW.SLIDESHARE.COM

WWW.TREECUTTINGLIFE.COM

WWW.QUORA.COM

WWW.REDDIT.COM

WWW.SAFETYCULTURE.COM

WWW.MANUALLIB.COM

WWW.INTRUCTABLES.COM

WWW.LAWNMOWERFORUM.COM

By exploring these resources and websites, you can gather valuable information about 2-stroke and 4-stroke chainsaws, compare different models, and make a well-informed decision based on your specific needs and preferences.

Two-Stroke Chainsaws Glossary:

1. **Priming**: The process of preparing the engine for starting by pumping fuel into the carburetor or combustion chamber.

2. **Full Choke**: A setting on the chainsaw that restricts the airflow to the carburetor, enriching the fuel mixture for easier starting.

3. **Burping the Engine**: A term used to describe the process of getting the engine to prime or start by pulling the starter cord a few times.

4. **Mixture Control Lever**: A lever on the chainsaw that controls the air-fuel mixture ratio going into the engine.

5. **Half Choke**: A setting that partially restricts the airflow to the carburetor, providing a richer fuel mixture for starting.

6. **Run Position**: The setting on the chainsaw where the air-fuel mixture is optimized for normal operation once the engine is running.

7. **Flooded Engine**: When there is an excess of fuel in the carburetor or combustion chamber, making it difficult to start the engine.

8. **Evaporation**: The process of liquid fuel turning into vapor and dissipating into the air.

9. **Combustion Chamber**: The part of the engine where the air-fuel mixture is compressed and ignited to generate power.

10. **Spark Plug**: An electrical component that ignites the air-fuel mixture in the combustion chamber to start the engine.

11. **Starter Cord**: A rope or cord used to manually start the engine by pulling it to turn the crankshaft.

12. **Piston**: The moving component inside the cylinder that compresses the air-fuel mixture and transfers power to the crankshaft.

13. Fuel reservoir: A container where gasoline is stored in a chainsaw.

14. Fuel filter: A device that removes impurities from the fuel before it reaches the engine.

15. Bar oil reservoir: A compartment where lubricating oil is stored for the chainsaw's bar and chain.

16. Safety glasses: Protective eyewear worn to shield the eyes from debris and potential hazards.

17. Volatile: Easily evaporating at normal temperatures and pressures, often used to describe substances that can ignite or explode.

18. Geyser: A sudden and forceful ejection of liquid, in this context, referring to fuel spurting out unexpectedly.

19. Pressure: The force applied perpendicular to the surface of an object per unit area.

20. Funnel: A conical utensil used to channel liquids into a container without spillage.

21. Overfilling: Filling a reservoir past its capacity, leading to spillage when closing the cap.

22. Snap-over/click: A locking mechanism that audibly confirms the closure of the reservoir cap.

23. Heating, stretching, and warping: Potential damage that can occur to the chainsaw's bar and chain if they become excessively hot or strained.

24. Chainsaw: A portable mechanical saw typically used for cutting wood.
Chainsaw Maintenance Glossary:

25. **Powerhead:** The main body of the chainsaw that houses the engine, fuel tank, and other essential components.

26. **Debris:** Accumulated dirt, wood chips, tree sap, bar oil, or fuel that can build up on the chainsaw during use.

27. **Heat Sink:** Material or substance that absorbs and dissipates heat to help prevent overheating of the chainsaw.

28. **Body Screws:** Fasteners used to secure various components of the chainsaw's body. Regularly checking and tightening these screws is essential for maintaining the chainsaw's structural integrity.

29. **Over-Tightening:** Applying too much force when tightening screws, which can lead to stripping of the threads and potential damage to the chainsaw.

30. **Spark Plug Boot:** Insulated covering that connects the spark plug to the ignition system, often disconnected during maintenance to prevent accidental starts.

31. **Starter Cord:** Rope used to manually start the chainsaw engine by pulling it through the starter mechanism.

32. **Fraying:** Damage to the cord characterized by unraveling or splitting fibers, commonly caused by repeated use and friction.

33. **Auto-Retractor:** Mechanism that automatically rewinds the starter cord after each use.

34. **Vented Cover Panel:** Removable panel on the chainsaw body that provides access to internal components, such as the starter cord retractor.

35. **Maintenance:** Regular tasks and checks performed to keep the chainsaw in optimal working condition and prevent potential issues. **Chain Maintenance Glossary:**

36. **Gullets:** The cutting surfaces of the teeth on a chainsaw chain.

37. **Round File:** A cylindrical file used for sharpening the cutting edges of chainsaw teeth.

38. **Rakers:** The depth gauges located in front of the cutting teeth on a chainsaw chain.

39. **Flat File:** A file with a flat surface used for leveling the rakers on a chainsaw chain.

40. **Bastard File:** A type of file with a coarse surface used for shaping and sharpening metal.

41. **Drive Links:** The part of the chainsaw chain that engages with the sprocket on the chainsaw's powerhead.

42. **Tensioning:** Adjusting the tightness of the chainsaw chain on the bar to ensure proper operation.

43. **Powerhead:** The main body of the chainsaw that houses the engine and other mechanical components.

44. **Sag:** The undesirable slack in a chainsaw chain that can affect cutting performance.

45. **Tip-to-Base Direction:** Refers to filing or sharpening motions that go from the tip to the base of the chainsaw tooth or raker.
Glossary:

46. Cover Plate: The protective plate on a chainsaw that covers and provides access to the internal components.

47. Debris: Loose particles or fragments, such as wood chips, sawdust, or oil residue, that accumulate inside the cover plate of a chainsaw.

48. Chip Deflector: A component on a chainsaw designed to redirect wood chips and debris away from the user during operation.

49. Bar Nuts: Nuts that secure the guide bar to the chainsaw body, typically found on the cover plate of the chainsaw.

50. Chain Catcher: A safety feature on a chainsaw designed to prevent the chain from hitting the user's hand and arm if it derails or breaks during operation.

51. E-clip: A small, circular retaining clip used to secure components in place on a chainsaw, typically found underneath the cover plate.

52. Axle Groove: A recessed channel in the axle of a chainsaw where the e-clip is inserted to hold components in position.

53. Scren014: A combination tool that functions as both a screwdriver and a wrench, commonly used for maintaining and adjusting chainsaws.

54. Serviceable: Capable of being repaired or maintained to ensure proper functionality.

55. Secure: Firmly fastened or attached to prevent movement or detachment during operation.

56. Reinsert: To put something back into its original position or location.

57. Contact Points: Areas where two components come into direct contact with each other, often requiring secure fastening for proper operation.

58. Washer: A flat, thin ring used to distribute the load of a threaded fastener, such as a bolt or nut, to prevent damage to the material being fastened.

59. E-clip: A type of retaining ring that fits into a groove on a shaft or bore to secure components in place.

60. Sprocket: A toothed wheel that engages with a chain or other perforated material, typically used to transmit motion or power.

61. Drive link grooves: The grooves on a sprocket where the drive links of a chain fit in, allowing the chain to rotate around the sprocket.

62. Chain brake: A safety feature on a chainsaw that stops the chain from moving, reducing the risk of injury.

63. Clutch drum: The component of a chainsaw that engages with the engine to drive the chain.

64. Debris: Small particles or fragments that can accumulate and obstruct the proper functioning of machinery.

65. Oiler worm: A mechanism that delivers oil to lubricate the chain and bar of a chainsaw.

66. Seating the drum: Ensuring that the clutch drum is correctly positioned and engaged with the oiler worm to facilitate proper oiling of the chain and bar.

67. Shearing: The process of breaking or cutting off a material, such as the gradual wear down of the oiler worm by the drum in a chainsaw.

68. Bar: The long, flat, and narrow guide on which the chain of a chainsaw moves.

69. Nose sprocket: The sprocket located at the tip of the guide bar that helps the chain rotate smoothly.

70. Grease injector: A tool used to apply grease to lubricate the nose sprocket for smooth operation.

71. Compressed air: Air that is under pressure, often used to clean and remove debris from machinery.

72. Tensioning: The process of adjusting the tension of the chain on the guide bar to ensure proper operation and safety.

73. Powerhead: The main body of the chainsaw that contains the engine and other components.

74. Bar nuts: Nuts used to secure the guide bar to the chainsaw body.

75. Throttle: A control that regulates the speed of the engine in a chainsaw.

76. Srench: A tool that combines a screwdriver and a wrench, typically used to tighten or loosen screws and bolts.

77. Vibrating loose: Refers to nuts or bolts that come loose due to the vibration of the chainsaw during operation.

How to leave a book rating or review on Amazon

1. Log into your Amazon account.
2. Go to the book title you want to rate/review
3. Select the number of stars you'd like to rate the book. If you'd like to just rate the book without leaving a review, go to step five.
4. Write a review in the Customer Reviews section. A review should be a minimum of 20 words and should tell other readers why they would like the book. (What did you like about it? What other books is it like?)
5. Click submit. Amazon will usually send you an email that lets you know your review was accepted.

Want to take it a step further?

Share your review on BookBub and Goodreads.

Thank You, Always on Your Side, Gaetano T Smith

On the next few pages, you will see an image of the other repair books that I created. Along with a link that you can copy it on a piece of paper, and then plug it into Amazon.com. Next, wait a short time and your book will be at your doorstep.

Outdoor Power Equipment Care and Repair, Part-1: Small Engine Guide:

https://www.amazon.com/dp/B0D2BQG198

Outdoor Power Equipment Care & Repair : Small Engine Guide Part-2 With A Question and Answer Section

https://www.amazon.com/dp/B0D4CTVM41

THANK YOU
ALWAYS ON YOUR SIDE,
YOUR SMALL ENGINE AUTHOR,
GAETANO T SMITH